THINK UNBROKEN:

8 Steps to Healing Your Inner Child

By: Michael Anthony

COPYRIGHT

Published by: Think Unbroken Book Publishing

ISBN: 978-1-7367766-1-2

Library of Congress Control Number: 2019920431

Written by: Michael Anthony
Front and back cover design by: Michael Anthony.
Back cover photo by: Aki Votrubová

DISCLAIMER

This book is not a replacement for seeking appropriate mental health care.

IF YOU OR SOMEONE YOU KNOW IS CURRENTLY EXPERIENCING A MENTAL HEALTH CRISIS AND NEED IMMEDIATE HELP PLEASE VISIT:
https://www.thinkunbroken.com/emergency-help-for-child-abuse

Or call your local emergency number.

DEDICATIONS

To Your Inner Child,

I see you. I feel you. I hear you.

You are not alone.

Inside of you is a warrior waiting to get out. Discovering self-love is without question the hardest thing that you may ever do.

When I ask myself what am I willing to do have have the life of my dreams, the answer is always WHATEVER IT TAKES.

By reading and accepting this new challenge of healing, you are one step closer to embodying the person you aspire to be.

This book offers the space to learn to love, heal, nurture, trust, and guide you if you are willing to put in the work. Even in the darkest of days, I know there is always a glimmer of light to guide us out of the darkness. May this book be your light.

I believe in you.

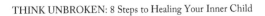

Though trauma may be our foundation, it is not
our future.

TABLE OF CONTENTS

INTRODUCTION

I remember the moment I realized I didn't understand what it meant to love myself. I was twenty-seven and had recently gotten serious about my trauma healing journey. Going to therapy regularly, working on mindset, learning how to eat well, quitting smoking and abusing alcohol, I believed I was on the path to healing; however, I kept falling backward and reverting to old patterns and behaviors. I was stuck in a loop of self-imposed chaos that I talk about in my first book, *Think Unbroken: Understanding and Overcoming*

Childhood Trauma. Let's just say that my childhood really fucked me up.

Sitting in my therapist's office on a bright, sunny Indiana summer afternoon, I wondered, What am I doing here? I kept going to therapy, but it felt like nothing was changing. There was always another visit, another payment, and another dive into the depths of my abuse. I felt like there must be more, and I continued to seek whatever that more could be, but I continually fell short. It seemed like I was destined to be trapped in The Vortex— the place in the mind where you can't seem to get yourself unstuck no matter what you do because you hate yourself, and the world has reinforced this through years of abuse.

In the midst of my frustration and despair, I finally decided to take therapy seriously for the first time. For years I had been going and paying all this money to tell my therapist what I thought they wanted to hear. Talk about the definition of insanity. Walking out of the therapy office to my car on that hot and humid Indiana day, I made a conscious choice to get serious and start speaking my truth, the real truth during my sessions. No more hiding from myself. I was so tired of feeling like a lost little boy. I was tired of feeling hurt, unloved, ashamed, guilty, and scared of my past and letting down the little boy in me.

I didn't understand at the time that this moment forever change my life. I wanted so desperately to *feel better,* but I had never been clear about why. I knew I needed to bridge the gap between what had happened to me and the man I now was because I was burning down my own house by standing in with matches in my hand, destroying everything around me as the child in me screamed, rescue me!

What I came to understand about myself and the world of childhood trauma, is that it is multifaceted and that to heal one part, you have to heal all parts, both past and present. **You have to heal your past.** I was **terrified** I would have to step into a place of comforting, protecting, and loving not only the Michael who was in the present moment but also the Michael who was that scared, terrified, helpless, unloved, and unprotected little boy. Talk about a mind fuck.

The truth about my experience in healing trauma is simple: If I didn't heal my past, I couldn't heal my present. And I will keep it real with you; I hated every single moment of healing my inner child, until I didn't.

I was engulfed in fear, resentment, guilt, and shame when I thought about the child version of myself. I would scoff at anyone who believed you should reach inside and hug the child version of you that was hurt. What bullshit. Or so I thought until a moment, during a deep meditation, when I held the hurt child in me and promised him that I would protect him.

The in-between of beginning to do that inner child work and the point in which I finally found the space to not only love but protect the child within me, took another five years of constant work. And as I did that work, I started to think more deeply about what it meant to love me, heal me, and be the Unbroken me writing this book today. I ultimately came to understand you have to protect and love the child in you in order to love the person you are today.

Take compassion with you as you step into the journey of healing your inner child. Healing your inner child is a process that no single book, podcast, or exercise can expedite. The only way this works is to **do the work,** day in and day out. That is the only secret I know about this process. You have to go towards love for yourself every day, and in time you will put your feet on the ground, and declare I LOVE ME.

In this book, you will find a short guide and framework to heal your inner child. There are hundreds of books on the subject and countless courses and seminars that you can attend. What is enclosed in the following pages of this book is what worked for me, and my only hope is that you will see that worked for me is not accidental but intentional and continues to guide me today.

I invite you to do three things as you read:

1. Challenge yourself. I know you may be thinking that just reading this book is already a challenge, and you would be correct, but in this journey, you will have to get vulnerable with yourself in ways that you may have never been before.

2. Be compassionate. The reality is that you have already suffered enough, and you don't need to add to your suffering. Ask yourself a straightforward question—How can I be kind to myself today?

3. Do the work. There are many suggestions in this book about what to do to start healing your inner child, but they are all just fruitless ideas if you do not follow through.

I want you to know that you are not alone in this process, and as someone who has been on the other side of these pages, I want to thank you for being willing to discover something new about yourself. No part of this healing journey is linear, but I do know that on a long enough timeline, everyone can Be Unbroken.

The path to healing requires daily effort and attention. There is no magical moment you no longer have to show up for yourself. I wish that weren't the truth, but it is. From this moment forward, you have to choose to be the HERO of your story.

I used to feel I was continually failing and falling backward, but I now see that wasn't true as I reflect on those experiences years later. Every day you grow and set a new precedent for who you are and what you are capable of. There is power in that truth and power in the reality that you start to heal the whole once you heal a piece.

The old negative behaviors and thought patterns are still present with me, and I don't know that they ever go away, but today they show up less often and hold less power. The inner turmoil, guilt, shame, hate, and disgust I had for myself have all but dissipated, and I hope that eventually, those dark parts never show up, but I can't promise you that reality. I can say that in learning to love myself both past and present, it has become clear that healing my inner child has given me so much space to be me without prejudice and with a little more compassion each day.

Though trauma may be our foundation, it is not our future.

-Michael

GETTING STARTED

I want to take a moment and say I really think you need to pause and pay close attention to what I am about to share with you. I challenge you to read this in solitude or, at least, find a space to let this information soak in.

In reflecting back on my experience and the work that went into my own healing, I keep coming back to the idea of healing the inner child. As I shared before, I initially thought the idea of healing the inner child was stupid, but I started to question why I felt that way I realized it was because I wasn't actually allowed to have a childhood. It was almost impossible for me to have a moment of peace, clarity, happiness, joy, or whatever that childlike wonderment is that so many people experience. As you may have experienced, coming from a home of abuse is not conducive to a great childhood.

As an adult, as I sat with knowing my childhood was stolen I started researching healing trauma, I kept seeing inner child, inner child, inner child. And the whole time, I thought to myself, well, this doesn't apply to me because I don't have a childhood, I don't have that experience, and I don't have that moment in time where I felt like—Oh, I'm a kid. This is childhood, this is happiness, this is peace, love, tenderness, and joy. And because of that, I just kept looking at this ideal of healing my inner child and it didn't make sense. Why would I go through the process of healing a childhood experience that I never had? And then I realized it is actually so incredibly important to understand that reconciling your childhood experiences is one of the most important cornerstones of this trauma–healing journey.

Perhaps I've done a really poor job to this point of actually relaying that to you. And to be fair, part of that is also because I feel like it's still a process that I am always exploring; I am always healing. And it's one of those things that even though I go, and

I learn, and I do certifications, and I have these sessions with myself in the world of trying to understand how to tap into my inner child. This journey is evolving, it's always changing, it's always growing. Being on this journey is about always trying to figure out how to step further into the place of healing of your inner child, or more importantly, I should say, my inner child. Yes, I am also writing this book for me. In part it's a reminder of what is possible, and in part it's a guide to develop tools we can incorporate into our toolbox.

As I'm in this, and as you're here with me, I am going to dive into this a little bit deeper than you have ever gone. I want to give you a little bit of clarity, hopefully—clarity about what healing your inner child means in your life. And so I put together this list of eight ways to step into the healing journey of your inner child. I want to tap into these steps with you, because right now, you're probably in a place in your life where, especially at this moment, you're thinking to yourself: "I have no idea what any of this means. This sounds nonsensical. What is my inner child? How do I do this?" Am I right? I have been there my friend, and I want to share that experience with you.

In my journey, these tools have been not only practical in changing the way that I think and feel about myself, but also, they have changed the way that I experience the world. Because I've been able to let down some of my guard and barriers that I had up for so long to protect myself, I have been able to become more vulnerable and compassionate towards myself.

In my book *Think Unbroken*, I shared that growing up, I wasn't allowed to cry, I wasn't allowed to explore my creativity, I wasn't allowed to nurture myself, and I wasn't allowed to even speak without ramifications. I understand that as you're reading this, you may be having memories or even flashbacks to those moments for yourself. And so, I want you to be very cautious when you're reading this book because it can be a little triggering. This book is not triggering in, i.e., I'm going to dive into my experiences because I don't think that's necessary. But as you're reading, you may have these moments where you think, Oh, this thing happened to me. So just a little heads-up, have yourself mentally prepared for stepping into healing. Again, we aren't going down the rabbit hole but I don't know how to talk about healing our inner child without talking about our experiences, including childhood.

WHO ARE YOU?

inner child—*noun:* a person's supposed original or true self, especially when regarded as damaged or concealed by negative childhood experiences.

-English Dictionary

Who am I? This must be the most challenging question a trauma survivor can attempt to answer. This question is so perplexing it may take a lifetime to craft a concrete statement. Who am I is a question I ask myself daily.

For the first twenty-five years of my life, I was living a lie. I was living as a hurt, lost, and unloved little boy. Two years ago I remember sitting on the train from London's Heathrow Airport into the city after living in Southeast Asia for the previous sixteen months. London was my next stop before heading back to America to see my brothers, sister, and friends. As I sat watching the street lights woosh by, I had a moment of clarity: I am finally me. I guess it would be unfair to say that I haven't always been me, but this was the first time I felt like me on my terms. As I glimpsed the brief reflections of my face in the window, I knew for sure that I was finally living life on my own terms.

How did I get here? My journey started with acknowledging my past, and accepting that dark things happened. There is no other way that I know to start this journey.

How did I find peace within my experiences of trauma, my choices as a man, and the fact that I would be facing this battle to heal for the rest of my life? In part, I recognized that I was fulfilling my visions of what I wanted my life to be, and the other part was that I was good with who I was. I was no longer afraid to say to myself—I love you, I'm proud of you, I see you.

I tried so many different modalities in healing my childhood trauma. Ultimately it was only in connecting with my inner child that the truth of who I am felt authentic and real. In that moment, I felt tremendous power in knowing I was good with the answer to the question—Who I am?

Let me explain.

I first want to talk about exactly who your inner child is and develop a commong understanding. If you are like me and come from a place where childhood was not allowed, finding and discovering who you were as a child will take some time. In my experience, it was really leveraging and looking at those moments when I felt at least some semblance of joy that started creating some indication for who I was as a child.

In my inital search for my inner child, I remembered that I loved building things. When I was young, I loved the idea of creating and building. I loved creating villages and communities with Legos and K'Nex. I was fascinated with putting objects together to make other objects. Not only did I remember my love for building but I also remembered I loved to write. I mentioned this in a podcast not too long ago: I wrote a vampire romantic comedy when like I was eight years old after seeing *Vampire in Brooklyn* and Anne Rice's, *Interview with the Vampire.* I remember writing a short story and thinkingI realized I am curious about writing, creating, and building.

As I've sat with this idea of naming who my inner child is, I've developed an understanding of him by tapping into these moments where I recognize, Okay, this is kind of who I identify with.

The hard part was I also had to identify the moments that weren't so fun and joyful, which obviously were the vast majority. I had to sit with those terrible experiences to be able to recognize and honor that I was a hurt, scared, shy little boy, who just wanted love and connection and companionship. I wanted to be seen and felt and heard. I wanted to be understood, hugged, kissed. I wanted to be told that I was good enough, strong enough, and that people were proud of me. That little boy was someone who really just wanted to be acknowledged for how great he was.

As a child, I knew that there was something remarkable about me. Still, I felt like there were always these barriers created by the adults in my life that kept me from being curious to discover what that greatness was. As an adult, I've had to identify who my inner child is—a scared, shy little boy— and mend that relationship within myself to tap into strength. I know you may listen to my podcast every week, have read my book *Think Unbroken,* seen the work that I do, and you may have even thought that what I do is courageous or that there's strength in it. The fact is there is strength and courage in what I do, and those same attributes are in you as well. Getting to a place that you can acknowledge your power is not easy—that is a hurdle, like for real—a hurdle that you have to leap over although it feels incredibly difficult and tedious. In time and with great patience, you will get there my friend.

As I stated before, you have to understand and befriend your inner child. If in the past they were that hurt, shy, scared, little boy or little girl, it's okay to acknowledge that. This is so important because in order to get to where we're going, we have to understand how we got to where we are. When I look at my inner child today I think, My inner child is a part of me that I protect, I nourish, I explore, and that I speak to truthfully and understand in this wonderful way. Being able to step into that level of connection has allowed me to explore the joy that is always available to me in my life. For example, when I need an emotional break from work, from life, from whatever, I will go and play video games for an hour or two, or three or four? Once every couple of weeks, once every couple of months, whenever that moment comes, I'm like, Okay, I need to honor that part of me that just needs to feel joy for a moment or play board games. I honor the part of my inner child that wants me to play more games. Playing more games was actually on my goals list for 2021. Being able to explore that joy is such a huge part of healing. Now, I will say that I am super competitive in it, but that's a part of who my inner child is as well. I want to compete. I want to win. I want to feel great about what I do.

Can you identify your inner child? What is it that you understand about who and what your inner child is?

Use this space to write who your inner child is:

-

FORGIVE YOURSELF

You have to forgive yourself.

Forgiving yourself is the most important and easily the most challenging thing you'll ever do in your life. There is power in acknowledging and knowing the truth: that the awful and traumatic events that happened to you as a child are **not your fault!** Nothing about the experience you've had growing up is your fault. You're not guilty of the bad things that happen to you. The people who were supposed to take care of you did not. They failed, not you. They are the responsible ones, not you, not 5-year old, 10-year old, 15-year old, or even 18-year old you. You are not responsible for those things. And you're going to have to come to peace with that shit. And I'm sorry, I wish it weren't true. I wish it weren't the case. But I have no fucking idea how you can move forward in life if you're still holding yourself accountable for other people's mistakes. So think about that for a moment. Can you forgive yourself? If you can't at this moment, what I want you to understand is this: It is not your fault. You cannot be responsible for shit you didn't do, got it? In no way can you be responsible for the rain; in the same way, you cannot be responsible for the sunshine. You just can't. And stop trying to find reasons why you could be responsible, because you're just stealing from yourself. That shit is fucking dark. It's ugly, it's unhealthy, and it will eat you alive.

You've got to be able to step ahead of that guilt. Forgiveness is so important in this healing journey. And look, I understand where you may still be stuck in that pattern, because I used to beat myself up every single day. I must have not been good enough; that's why my birth father was never in my life. I must be a loser; that's why those beatings happened. And so on. We all create our own stories all the time. And I've said it a million times: We are the stories that we tell ourselves. Start telling yourself a different story. You owe it to yourself. You owe yourself foregiveness for the shit you didn't do, period.

If someone throws garbage in your front yard, you can either step over it every day and pretend it's not there, or you clean it up. The sad truth about this is we are often left cleaning up other people's mistakes.

One practical tool that worked exceptionally well for me was creating an inner dialog with my inner child. I would sit alone in silence and visualize telling the child in me that what happened wasn't their fault. I'll be honest, this was incredibly difficult at first, and as you will read later, it was a precursor for a massive shift in my life. I know that you might be reading this and thinking the very prospect of speaking to your inner child is stupid, but if you are willing to step into it, you will see change.

Think about what it would mean to forgive yourself. What would happen if you took away the shame and guilt you feel for your childhood experiences that you were never in control of? Would you feel a sense of relief, excitement, or hope?

Write what your life would look and feel like if you forgave yourself for things that are not your fault:

EXPLORE

Exploring is one of my favorite things about healing your inner child. For many of us, we can give ourselves permission to play for the first time. When we're young, the creativity within exploration is often met with judgment. We are forced to draw inside the lines, color inside the lines, build our life like theirs, and we continuously hear, *Don't you dare go outside of the box.*

I want you to think about the impact that conformity has had culturally and socially in the world. Now think about how regardless of childhood experiences, that by-the-numbers mentality has limited society. There's no space to be creative because the second you do, someone's going to pick on you, someone's going to judge you, someone's going to bully you. So as an adult, you have to make adult choices, and guess what? You get to shut those people out. People who want to bring you down don't get a say; they don't get a place at your table.

Can you explore creativity? And more importantly, can you do this without judging yourself? What is your inner child curious about? What is it that you want to know in the world? If you're going to heal your inner child, step into creativity and exploration of every kind. If you're going to get in touch with your inner child, do it without judgment. Think about this: how often as a kid were you curious about something in the world only to have it shut down by adults, peers, or the people around you? More often than not, I would guess. You aren't a child anymore! I say fuck that and fuck them. Step into what you are curious about. What is it that **you** want to explore? I know this very concept of choice and agency can be unnerving. Still, the reality is that you are allowed to do whatever you can imagine and will allow yourself to do!

Every day I think about the concept of Thinking Unbroken: understanding and overcoming childhood trauma to become the hero of your own story. This book is the result of me taking the

things that I was curious about as a child—
building, creating, writing, and making it come to
fruition. And look, I get judgment every day.
People judge me every single day. I say let them.
Fuck 'em. There is real power in moving towards
the what sparks curiousity and nurtures creativity.
They judge me, but I don't judge myself. Can you
step into that? Can you look into what it is that
you're curious about and not judge yourself?

If you're struggling with how to figure this
exploration part out, start with baby steps. It's
totally fine to just tap your toe in the water and say,
"Okay, this is interesting."

Get curious about your inner child first by asking yourself some questions to figure out what your inner child wants.

Ask yourself:

- Do I want to paint?
- Do I want to draw?
- Do I want to write poetry?
- Do I want to just go lie in the grass and stare at the stars at night?
- Do I want to climb a tree?
- Do I want to do whatever it is that I want to do?

And then, the most important part, can you do these things you are curious about exploring without judging yourself? That inner voice in your head will say, You're a grown-up. You're an adult. Do the grown-up things, do the adult things. Ignore it. Go live your life, go be creative, go explore!

We are told from a very young age to be afraid of everything, and that idea gets reinforced in our home environment. The hardest thing about healing your inner child and childhood trauma is, I think, coming to terms with the fact that the world is actually not as scary as we think it is. To know the world as a dangerous place is a truth you come by honestly. Fear has been reinforced time and again in your experiences. The idea that you should be terrified of the world is a hypothesis that has been proven true too many times ... and I can't help but laugh because it's my experience as well.

I come from a place where people don't have passports, where they don't leave the neighborhood, where we die on the same street we grew up, we get arrested going to school, and where we watch drugs and poverty destroy everything around us. One of my greatest achievements is healing trauma and healing my inner child, and doing it through challenging myself to explore. I'm writing this as I'm sitting in Mexico, and for that, I am proud. I never thought I would make it out of my neighborhood, and now I've traveled the world and back again. I never anticipated I would see the world and get to experience it because I was so fearful. And now, I look at the world through the lens of someone who has explored it because they needed to know what lived on the other side of discomfort. I can tell you that to push yourself into what you are curious about is real healing. I know with certainty and having ventured around the world, that the world is not as scary as people would have us believe it is. I wouldn't discovered that truth had I not connected with the curiousity of my inner child. My inner child wondered, What it was like to be on an airplane?

Explore your inner child, what they want, and just go for it! Exploring your inner child may mean getting out of your own neighborhood, crossing the state line, getting on a train or a plane for the first time, buying that passport, going to that country, doing that thing which can even seem frightening.

I'll tell you this, if you're willing to step into the world without fear, you're going to learn how to explore your inner child. I know that sounds weird. And you're probably thinking, How do those things connect? Think about when you were young. You would explore everything, your house, your neighborhood, the weird creek in the back yard, the park at night—whatever that was, you were always exploring and seeking. Then you grow up, learn a lot of terrifying truths about the world, and find yourself frozen. Everything will reinforce the idea you are not allowed to explore the world without being afraid. But my friend, I'm here to tell you, it's simply not true. Trust me.

I think about the power of hope and how it can be such a fantastic catalyst for tapping into possibility. Can you explore hope, the idea of hope, the concept of hope, the word hope? Can you apply meaning to it and how it exists in your life while stepping into exploration?

Hope, just like everything else I've learned recently, is about exploring. I believe hope is a beautiful catalyst for creating change in your life. Because we need something to hold on to at baseline, we need an idea, we need a concept, we need something beyond us that pushes us to continue to tap into the power we have inside. And hope is such an excellent catalyst for power not only in healing your inner child but in life. When you measure yourself with the idea of possibility and consider, Okay, if I have a little bit of hope, then something on the other side of this action, idea, work, concept, will be different. That's power!

As a child, the only hope I truly ever had was the hope to make it out alive. As an adult my hope is different. When I connect with that lost, scared, helpless little boy in me, I hope that all his dreams come true. I continue to heal my inner child and **do the work**. Even today, writing this, all I ever think about is making my dreams come true. Because why not? I deserve it. And you deserve whatever it is that you want in your life. You have to earn it, but it's worth the effort. I don't know if all of my dreams will happen, but I hope they will, and I do the work every day. On a long enough timeline, my hope of eradicating childhood trauma and abuse in the world will see the light. I don't know if it will happen in my lifetime. But I hope that it will, so I keep moving forward every single day.

Can you define what hope means in healing your inner child? Can you explain what hope means in your life in general? Can you explore exploration?

Use this space to answer these questions:

NURTURE YOUR NEEDS

I had no idea how to take care of myself beyond the bits and pieces I had picked up from watching other people. I knew to brush my teeth and drink water, but I didn't know how to set boundaries, say no, or put myself first. For decades I felt this constant battle with myself, comparing who I was in the moment with who I wanted to become and what I thought I should be doing. The more I began to heal, the more I began to feel a sense of loneliness creeping in. Deep into the process, I found myself doing everything from EMDR (Eye Movement Desensitization and Reprocessing) to Reiki and everything in between. Despite becoming healthier, I still felt so alone in all of it. And worse, I didn't know if I was actually taking care of myself. I was desperately seeking companionship and community but ironically I was so lonely I was also missing what was right in front of my face. Getting caught up in the day-to-day—I'm on an inner child healing journey—can get both cumbersome and isolating, which leaves much room for ideation.

It was a cold and rainy spring afternoon in Portland. As I sat in my therapist's office, I had a moment of enlightenment that was six years in the making. I told him how much I hated coming into his office every Wednesday and how I hated that I was the one doing trauma work for shit that wasn't my fault. It wasn't a volatile exchange but it wasn't happy either.

As I sat in the back-and-forth of my loathing for trauma healing and his patience in being there to welcome my angst, he said something that would change my life.

"You can be depressed and still tend to your garden." The words felt like a warm blanket, a hug from someone you love, or an ice-cold lemonade; they were the comfort I needed at that moment.

It was suddenly clear to me that it was perfectly OK to be in the throes of healing and still long for the basic comforts one needs as a human being. That moment sitting across from my therapist was such an essential catalyst for change because until that moment, no one had told me that I was allowed to be an emotional human being, put my needs first, and live my life.

I recognize that as you are in the process of healing your inner child, this idea of nurturing yourself feels scary. Nurturing yourself—think about that, have you ever once in your life been told that nurturing yourself is allowed? I'm going to guess probably not. Think about what the word nurture means in healing trauma and healing your inner child—**nurture: the process of caring for and encouraging the growth or development of someone or something**. The care, compassion, love, and admiration that you as a child did not get are the care, compassion, love, and admiration you deserved and should have had. Today you have to nurture yourself; there is no way around it and no one will do it for you. Healing your inner child means that you have to nurture your needs. Ask yourself, what do you actually need? What can you do in your life to make it more sustainable, joyful, or feel more alive? What is going to bring you to the present moment? **What do you need?** Can you nurture that feeling inside of you to take care of yourself without judgment?

We are often terrified of the idea that it's okay to take care of ourselves. I don't have another way to put this; if you aren't nurturing your needs, you're not going to be able to heal your inner child. You are essentially learning to reparent yourself.

The most simplified way to explain reparenting is to do what your parents should have done the right way. From compassion and love to boundaries and rules, you will have to be the person to take care of you.

If you need to step into healing your inner child, which you probably do, because realistically we all do, then you need to be willing to nurture the needs that come up as you're in the process. You must nurture the need for self-care, the need for defining your wants, needs, interests, personal boundaries, and values. I went in-depth on this in my book *Think Unbroken: Understanding and Overcoming Childhood Trauma.*

All of your needs deserve to be met, and you have to choose to do that through nurturing yourself. As you begin to put yourself first in life, the journey often takes gigantic leaps of faith. The truth is, if and when you are willing to take those leaps, you will see enormous change, but only on the other side of it all.

I want you to think about moments in your life when you put yourself first and took care of yourself before others because you needed to. How did that feel? Empowering? We get lost in always putting ourselves second as trauma survivors because that has been our experience until this moment. We have learned through our experiences that we are less-than, which is one of the most unfair truths of abuse. Today you have a choice to make. Can you be first in your life and take care of what needs to be taken care of?

I go back to the notion of tending my garden, and the thought that sits with me as I reflect is that it is perfectly fine to take care of yourself even when (and especially) when life seems to be smashing your spirit into the ground. My hope for you is that you understand something straightforward in these words: you are allowed to take care of yourself and still be hurt, sad, angry, depressed, happy, loved, joyful, or any other human emotion that you feel.

What does it mean to you to nurture yourself?
What would life feel like if you put yourself first?
What is one thing that you can do today to take
care of yourself?

Use this space below to answer the questions:

SPEAK YOUR TRUTH

There is nothing that I know better than not being allowed to be me. For most of my childhood, I existed within the space of being invisible. You have likely heard the notion that children are to be seen and not heard. Maybe you experienced this in your home? There was nothing more threatening to my existence than the moment I would break protocol by being myself. Just the idea that I would dare have a thought or opinion would get me slammed to the ground, locked in a room overnight, berated, belittled, demeaned, hurt, beat, or worse. As it is true that everything we experience in life shapes us, then you have to consider that the reality of the events in your life that left you feeling like less than a human has carried over into this moment. The problem with learning to be invisible is that for a time, it serves us, it protects us, it keeps us hidden from pain and suffering, and that is a mechanism for survival—until it isn't.

The power we hold in coming into our voice is something that I can't fully express in words. For me this looks like, standing up for myself and tapping into my sovereignty. Against what everyone may think, I move towards things that serve me, for me. The part of us that is controlled deeply by fear tells us not to show up as we are, because there will be ramifications. This fear served us by keeping us safe during childhood and throughout the abuse. This coping mechanism works well until you recognize that living in fear impedes your ability to be great or love yourself and others fully.

The moment I gave myself permission to use my voice, stand up for myself, be the person I am, and live according to my values, was the greatest moment and decision I have ever made. The decision to be me came with fear and a lot of it, but at some point, I had to ask myself, What was I really afraid of? I came to understand that people will always judge you, people will always tell you that you aren't enough, and they will always be the first to say—I told you so—when you fail. You know what I say to those people in return? Nothing. They don't get to sit at my table.

Speaking your truth and healing your inner child is a beautiful experience that I hope everyone who has experienced pain will have. Once you start to step into yourself, this becomes more real; you effectively become more present with the idea that you have an inner child. Your truth helps solidify that newfound understanding of self. I think of these three truths regarding healing your inner child and doing trauma work in general—can you get to the place where you can say, I love you, I hear you, and thank you?

I love you is so important. Because if you're not going to say it to yourself, who will? I know that is so hard to get to that place, especially when you feel like you've never been deserving of love, or love was taken away or stripped from you, or on the backside of love, there was always some kind of consequence or penalty or payment, and worst of all you may had to earn love in some way. I believe that you have to earn love throughout inner child work, and many people will disagree with me on this, and that's fine. But I believe that you do have to earn love for yourself. Earning love for yourself means doing the right things right by going inward, creating it, and earning it. My experience was very much in being stuck in this place where I hated myself. And you may relate to that. You may be reading this right now and saying, I fucking hate myself. I get it, and I'm sorry because you deserve more.

You have to speak your truth of love into yourself and the world. I imagine bringing light to this inner child work, and this isn't woo-woo, but it's true; you have to put your love into the universe. Darkness surrounds us all the time, especially when we are in this awfully negative mindset. When we feel depressed, anxious, hurt, suicidal—I get it, I have been there, I have worn every one of those hats. If there is something awful one can say to oneself, I assure you I have said it.

Now I wake up every day and put my feet on the ground with gratitude. And I think to myself how much I love myself, for all the effort, all the work. Healing your inner child through saying, I love you, isn't easy. I know it isn't easy, and in fact, it's so incredibly hard most people quit before even mouthing the words: I love my inner child. You are the one who gets to define what love means. And with that power, you get to step into understanding yourself in a way you never have, which is beautiful and empowering.

To be able to sit within your inner child and say—I love you—is you taking your power back! I know without question you can create self-love, but you're going to have to earn it. Creating self-love may start with compassion, but it may also start with doing hard things, building yourself back up, holding yourself accountable, going to the course, taking the class. Speak that truth into yourself every single day! Not sure how? Stand in front of a mirror, and look at yourself and say, I love me. I love myself. Speak your truth—I love you, I hear you, I see you. Mirror work in healing your inner child can play such a pivotal role in this self-love process.

Stepping into self-love is important because we often ignore our needs. We find power in coming back to nurturing our needs. You have to speak aloud about the things you need, want, and are interested or curious about. Put your power into the universe and then write it down. Take a piece of paper and write down what it is that you need. Speak that truth. Create that reality. What is it within you that needs to come out? Stop holding it in. Suppose you want to heal your inner child. In that case, if you're going to step out of this trauma, you will have to acknowledge your desires, needs, interests, personal boundaries, goals, and hobbies. Whatever they are, you're going to have to say them aloud. You're going to have to put it into the universe because the more you do, the more it starts to become comfortable. And the more it becomes comfortable, the more you begin to own it. And the more that you own it, the more it starts to become who you are. And eventually, one day, you're going to look in the mirror, and you're going to say, Oh, I'm the person that I always thought I could be.

The truth about getting to the place of loving yourself is that it's odd at first. You can start to find peace by taking action and thanking yourself for doing the work. Say thank you to your inner child, to the current you, to the adult you are in this moment. Say thank you! This shit is fucking hard. No part about this life, about this journey, about healing, about overcoming trauma, about becoming the hero of your own story, about anything we do to make our lives better is easy.

Healing your inner child is not a walk in the park, and if it were, you wouldn't be reading this right now, and you sure as hell wouldn't have made it this far without some serious effort. So thank yourself, acknowledge yourself, give yourself accolades, and more importantly, especially as you're healing your inner child, give that inner child thanks. Say, Thank you for surviving, thank you for finding a way to be resilient. Thank you for showing up, even though it was so challenging. Thank you for trying to make it every day. Thank you for doing all this hard shit that you shouldn't have to do. There's power in these statements about gratitude, my friend. I'm telling you to own this moment. There is so much beautiful power in the idea of thanking yourself. Expressing gratitude acknowledges the reality that you've been through some hard shit. And you deserve to feel some gratitude.

What is it that you are thankful for on your inner child healing journey?

Use the space below to write what you are thankful for:

A LETTER TO YOURSELF

I kept coming across people who spoke about writing a letter to the inner child. What nonsense I thought. Why would I do something so silly? The very idea of writing a letter to myself felt asinine and I don't really know why. I did know that if all these people were saying it worked, then maybe I needed to get out of my own way. As you are reading this, you may be wondering why it is healing to write a letter to your inner child.

I'll be forthright here. It wasn't until I actually made a declaration to myself one evening as I sat listening to an audiobook on healing childhood trauma that I would finally just write the damn letter to myself. In writing that letter, I discovered its power. I don't think I have the words to convey the inner struggle I faced with writing my letter. In fact, I'd rather doing anything else, but I made a choice. Part of healing my inner child was holding to and following through on my decisions, so I had to do it.

As I wrote, line by line, I felt a sense of intense anger and frustration. Much like that day in my therapist's office, a sense of, Why the hell do I have to do this? came over me. I was mad about having to do another healing trauma exercise that I didn't want to do. But I did it because I said I would. I kept a promise to myself, which in hindsight was more difficult than the actual writing.

Once I finished, I read the letter back to myself. The lines were filled with words that conveyed both my anger and frustration and my hope and admiration for my childhood experiences. I felt a sense of hope and pride in those words. As I had many times before, I also promised myself that I would protect my inner child because if I didn't, who else would?

Today, as I reflect on that evening and the words on that piece of paper, I am proud of myself for doing one of the most uncomfortable things I had done up to that point. I did it because I asked myself: **What am I willing to do to have the life**

that I want to have? Ultimately, we are faced with having to follow through on our promises to ourselves. On the backside of those promises, more often than not, something beautiful comes, like a tool that we can reach for in our darkest hour.

Write yourself a letter and a promise, because there will be a time when it might save you. Writing your inner child a letter is a tool; realistically, that's what it is. It is a tool that you will leverage in the moments you need to the power and strength to get you through obstacles and roadblocks. You may be asking yourself, Well, what kind of letter do I write to my inner child? What kind of promise do I make to my inner child? The letter's content is for you to decide. It can be a combination of all the things you have been reading about or totally different. Ultimately, it's about creating something practical that is a tool you can leverage and a reminder in those moments of doubt.

In my coaching sessions, I always have my clients do this exercise. In their journey with me, they're going to have to write a promise to themselves, something that undeniably cannot be broken, period. I have them write letters to themselves because I know the power our own words can have when we need them.

I've done this work myself. And I have a letter right now in my hand, and I keep it on Google Drive, so it's always there when I need it. And it's there as a leverage point and tool for those moments in which I feel weak. That letter to my inner child at one point was such a practical tool that I was reading it regularly. Then I would revamp it because I'm always growing, healing, changing. In the process of change, I'm always looking at how I make my letter to my inner child more in tune with what I'm going to need next?

As I write, I'm thinking about mitigating the risks of childhood trauma and the ramifications that came along with abuse. By having this tool in my belt, during those moments in which this challenge of healing childhood trauma is the most difficult or I'm letting myself down, or I'm not showing up, or in The Vortex, I take out that letter and read it. I read that letter to my inner child because it is a catalyst as a reminder and a kick in my own ass that reminds me, **Go and do the fucking things that you said you're going to do.** Stop letting yourself down, stop being a fucking loser! These are **my** words. Let me be super clear; this is how **I** talk to myself because this is what **I** need to pump myself up. If this isn't your vibe, and you need to be the most courteous and kind person ever to your inner child, please do that. I have done that work, and I am in a different place now. So let me be clear, I need a kick in the ass. I don't need a hug most of the time. Of course, I will always take a hug because I'm super comfortable with the idea that that is okay in my life.

My letter to my inner child is about motivating myself. It guides me when I need that intrinsic push to go further, to go harder, to continue down the path, in the times where it's hard, where it's rough, where it's difficult, where I want to give up, where I'm mad at myself, or I am angry at the world, where my emotion starts to take over, or whatever it is, that letter is there for me. I read that letter to my inner child as a way of healing. This healing your inner child work is a continuum.

Healing is a process, and growing despite abuse is going to take the rest of our lives.

Create your letter to your inner child, write it, and put it somewhere you can access it when you need it most. If it's about forgiving yourself, if it's about stepping into hope, if it's about creating goals and a game plan, whatever that inner child letter is, write it and put it somewhere because you will need it. This needs to be a letter that you physically create. You have to write this.

Writing is a practice and a form of speaking truth. If you do anything I have suggested in this book, make it this. Write your inner child a letter on paper first, then copy it over into your Google

Drive or wherever it's accessible, or put it on a note on your phone. The location doesn't matter. Put it somewhere that you can have it when you need it. And then when you need that moment, when your inner child needs love, when you need to step further into healing when you feel like your back is against the wall, go and read that letter. And I promise you, I promise you—it will change where you are.

Use this space to write your inner child a letter of power, strength, hope, trust, forgiveness, thanks, gratitude, or love:

MEDITATION

For a very long time, I was paralyzed by the idea of meditation as a form of healing my childhood trauma. It felt terrifying to be alone with my thoughts. I would tiptoe into the practice of meditation on occasion. Still more often than not, I would feel more anxious and scared than when I started the meditation.

About five years ago, I was in a random Holiday Inn in Salt Lake City, Utah, having my third panic attack of the day. These panic attacks would come from nowhere and cripple me. For days I would be perfectly fine, and then suddenly, the world would start caving in on me. As I laid down on that dirty patterned carpet reminding myself that I wasn't dying, I had a moment of clarity. What if I could force my brain to stop this? I thought to myself.

I picked myself off the floor, reached for my phone, and googled: how to stop panic attacks meditation. I clicked the first video that came up. What happened next blew my mind, literally. I put my earbuds in, listened to the thirty-minute guided meditation, and discovered something extraordinary about the human brain. Adaptation for survival is its only goal. As I listened, I understood that I could, at least to some extent, control my brain—a thought I had never had before.

I listened patiently as the guide told me to imagine I was walking down a brick path to a lush green garden. He told me to feel the sun on my face and to smell the flowers. He guided me to lay in the grass and to breathe. And then he said, "Allow the panic attack to happen. Stop trying to control everything. Let this pain escape you." Talk about a holy shit moment!

What he said felt spot on because I understood that I had been holding on too tight. For years I had been white-knuckling life at every turn. Even when my life was a disaster, I was holding onto that steering wheel for dear life. In hearing his words, it became clear that sometimes you just have to let go.

I kept diving deeper into guided meditations and eventually started guiding myself through meditation. This took years of practice, and now meditation has become a daily routine. The fantastic thing about meditation is that it works, but it does take time and practice. As I write this, it has been years since I sat in that hotel listening to that panic attack meditation, and I can count on two hands how many panic attacks I have had.

Meditation became another tool for healing my inner child because I realized that if I could apply meditation to panic attacks, it must work for other areas of my life. I was right.

Our subsconcious drives our decision-making process. I think we don't fully recognize that by witnessing our subsconscious thought patterns in meditation we allow for the possibility of relinquishing control and relaxing. Being able to tap into the subconscious and surrender control through meditation is a truth that needs to be shared with the world.

No question meditating is part of inner child healing work. Meditation can vary for you , but I am going to share an approach that might be useful. I step into meditation with intention and purpose. I say to myself, If I'm going to step into meditation around inner child work, then I'm going to do it intentionally because I can use this tool to make my life better. I do it like that because I want to know exactly what's happening when I'm stepping into that moment of presence within myself. I take myself to a place of comfort because looking inward can be scary.

If you've happened to listen to the Michael Unbroken podcast long enough, you know one of the very early episodes was about the experiences I had with psilocybin and healing my inner child. While doing a hero dose of psilocybin in a float tank, I came to understand I was going to be the protector of my inner child. That experience of using plant medicine for healing my childhood trauma was a catalyst for this lovely moment of change in my life. Still I want to point out that that moment was preceded by years of meditation. I wanted to get comfortable within my own thoughts. I wanted to know that place of peace and calm and quiet, which can be terrifying for many people, especially when you've experienced trauma. And so you baby step your way into it like you do everything else in trauma healing. There is no reason to deep dive into the unknown when it comes to creating an understanding of who you are. You start off simply with a little patience and grace.

After years of using meditation as a tool for healing my inner child, I know there is no right or wrong way to meditate. Meditation, like everything, is a practice, and if you can practice for 30 seconds, or one minute, or five minutes, or twenty, that is where you start and watch what happens. Meditation for healing trauma is not about the destination; it's about the practice and the challenge of learning something new about yourself through doing something uncomfortable. Meditation can be as simple as: Can I be present with myself for one minute, no distractions, no phone, no email, no text, no music, no nothing, just the peace and quiet within myself by myself?

When healing your inner child, meditation can help you get to that place where you find the confidence it takes to do the hard things. I think people rush this meditation thing way too quickly, and it's problematic. I wouldn't go scuba diving without having ever been in a pool.

With patience and practice, you will find the confidence to get closer to tapping into the inner child during meditation. As you slowly get more aware and more cognizant of yourself and your subconscious, you will have a better framework and understanding of how your mind works. As you continue to meditate you will likely find the way to start speaking to yourself—that inner child—in a way that is nurturing, compassionate healing, loving and kind. Ultimately you may even find yourself saying, I will protect my inner child, I will protect myself, I will be the hero of my own story. That was my experience. Yours might be different. That's how I got to that moment with psilocybin. By taking this intense dive into becoming comfortable with the silence of self-discovery, I have comforted my subconscious inner child.

HONOR YOUR JOURNEY

When am I healed? is the number one question I used to ask myself. How long do I have to do this trauma healing shit? is number two.

I felt so lost in the process of healing because I just wanted it to be done. Why couldn't there be an ending to all this? It seemed like every time I learned more about my inner child, the science of trauma, or the power I was discovering, the more that I came closer to understanding the truth: this journey doesn't end.

In one sense, knowing that this trauma healing challenge is a life-long venture is freeing because I can adapt to knowing that this work is a part of who I am now. On the other hand, it fucking sucks. I would love to be entirely free of all of this, but I don't know if that moment is in the cards. That's not to say that trauma and my past rules everything around me, it doesn't. It is also true that most days I don't get to pretend my trauma is not there.

I found freedom and compassion for myself when I was able to accept my fate as a trauma survivor and warrior. It almost feels dark writing that, but the truth is acceptance is freeing.

Today as I sit with the understanding of who I am in hope and courage, despite my childhood trauma, I feel the overwhelming emotion of pride for being on this journey when the easiest thing to do was quit.

Honoring your journey in healing your inner child is about recognizing yourself for the effort you put into your own life. This means nurturing yourself, speaking your truth, writing the letter, meditation, exploring, forgiving yourself, and understanding. Honoring the journey to me, is about continuing to show up every day, just going for it, learning, and stepping into it. Owning, thinking, healing, growing, and everything in between **is the work.** Honoring your journey is about looking at your life from an unbiased perspective and saying to yourself, Yeah, I'm in this right now. This is happening. This is my life. I have control over this moment. This is my choice. I am the one in power, not them. Not the past, not twenty-five fucking years ago, right now, at this moment, I am the hero of my own story. This is what it means to honor your journey as you show up for yourself and your inner child.

You may recognize at this moment, even by being here right now, reading and owning this that you are on the journey. **Honor that truth.** Own it. Recognize that even in the moments you step back, and in the moments where you fuck up, and in the moments when things aren't what you thought or excepted them to be, that you are still on this journey. This is a forever thing. When you understand healing trauma and healing your inner child is a game of patience and a lifelong endeavour, you start to take your power back. Understand that everyday you're in the healing work; this is the journey, this is the moment, **this is your life.**

What can you honor about your journey?
Use this space to write what honoring yourself
looks like and means to you:

THANK YOU

My friend, thank you so much for being a part of this, for stepping into healing your inner child, for being willing to do the work, for looking at life through the lens of someone who wants to be better. I honor you, and I celebrate this inner child healing journey because it's hard. I'm sorry that we have to do this. I'm sorry that we have to have this conversation. I'm sorry that I have to write this book and that you have to read it, but I'm proud of both of us for being here. We are cleaning up the garbage in our front yard, and because of the work that we are doing, we are taking steps to end generational trauma and heal our own inner child.

I wish that we could connect in literally any other way you could imagine. But **this is our truth.** This is our journey.

We are in this together.

Know this, as you are healing your inner child and as you are working through trauma, **you are not alone.**

Though trauma may be our foundation, it is not our future.

Until next time…

Be Unbroken,
Michael

NO EXCUSES.

JUST RESULTS.

REVIEW

Your review would mean the world to me. Please take two minutes and leave a review about this book through the store or platform you purchased it from. I would love your genuine and honest thoughts about this book, so that I can learn how to become a better author but also because it is important to me that as a community, we can come together and create better information for other trauma warriors on their healing journey.

CONTACT

I am here to support you on your journey to health, healing, happiness, success, love, longevity, and everything in between. You are not alone on this mission.

Email: Michael@ThinkUnbroken.com

Podcast: Listen to **The Michael Unbroken Podcast** on iTunes and Spotify

Instagram: @MichaelUnbroken and @ThinkUnbroken

Facebook: www.facebook.com/MichaelUnbroken

Coaching: www.ThinkUnbroken.com

30-Day Trauma Healing Challenge:

www.HealTraumaCoach.com

ABOUT THE AUTHOR

Michael Anthony is the author of the best-selling book *Think Unbroken: Understanding and Overcoming Childhood Trauma.* He is a coach, mentor, and educator for adult survivors of child abuse. Michael spends his time helping other survivors get out of The Vortex to become the hero of their own story and take their lives back.

Michael hosts The Michael Unbroken podcast, teaches at Think Unbroken Academy, and is on a mission to create change in the world. For more information visit: www.ThinkUnbroken.com

BY: MICHAEL ANTHONY

Think Unbroken: Understanding and Overcoming Childhood Trauma

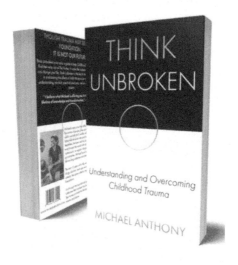

Think Unbroken: Understanding and Overcoming Childhood Trauma is not only a guide to helping other Trauma Survivors find their way out of The Vortex, but it is also the cornerstone to how I changed my life. I am, in essence, a product of my product, and I believe that Think Unbroken is the key to taking the first steps in overcoming the effects of childhood trauma.

This book will expose you to possibility through mindset, palatable understandings of self, and a step-by-step guide to discovering out how to place the first piece of the puzzle on the table.

What you will find in *Think Unbroken: Understanding and Healing Childhood Trauma*, is not just my story, but a reflection of the possibilities that can become a reality when you understand that mindset is everything. Childhood trauma took everything from me, but I took everything back, and so can you.

Available at www.ThinkUnbroken.com and wherever books are sold.

NOTES:

NOTES:

NOTES:

NOTES:

NOTES:

NOTES:

NOTES: